unlearning is a transformative process
to re-discover who you are. and once
you uncover even the slightest glimpse
you'll have to undress yourself yet again
and go deeper further far beyond where
you're prepared to go. for there really
is no there. just more to unpack. more
to uproot. to turn. to plow. if you
really wanna be free, the journey
of self-awareness will set you aflame.
and this fire ain't for the faint of heart.
-- *adrian michael*

in dedication to
claude harris jr.
a true example
of what it really means
to be a man.

he was taught to be this way.

i (in this) is the collective we. i, step in and out of observation and experience. shifting bodies. jumping galaxies. traversing different worlds. what is personal and what is general is not important here. (what is) important is both singular and universal. pieces. part of the whole. both journal and journalism. expository and narrative. i, a complex simpleton, comprised of the words and deeds past of myself. of others. moments in a mirror. i, bare with answers, come with possible truths (pebbles from mountains) recording my (our) voice. poetics of a man.

-- him, 2018
berkeley, california

TITLES YOU MIGHT LIKE
BY
ADRIAN MICHAEL

--

loamexpressions

blinking cursor

notes of a denver native son

blackmagic

lovehues

notes from a gentle man

blooming hearts

book of her book of she

for hearts that ache.

he was taught to be this way. I + II

Published by Creative Genius Publishing—
an imprint of lovasté

I Denver, CO I Berkeley, CA I

To contact the author visit adrianmichaelgreen.com
Book jacket designed by Adrian Michael Green
Back cover photo courtesy of Eliott Foust

ISBN-13: 978-1974614271
ISBN-10: 1974614271

Printed in the United States of America

he was taught to be this way.

the purpose of this book

+++

the purpose of this book is to help men become better men and for women to better understand men. it is not about shaming men. it is about being in constant conversation with masculinity and bringing awareness to the conscious and unconscious things that men do in and out of relationships. it is about shedding light on all dimensions into journeying into a process of becoming/being a good man and defining what being a man really means to you.

framework: *he was taught to be this way.* uses the *king, warrior, magician, lover* manhood framework that pyschologists gilette and moore derived from the work of carl jung as a way to categorize and center the hundreds of responses (questions and stories) people have shared with me over the last five years and were placed into either the kwml sections of this book to spark discovery and growth. many topics addressed in this volume could easily have been placed in either quadrant and crossover into multiple archetypes but understand that i have deemed their primary function to exist mostly in its current placement.

understanding the setup: on most pages you will find topics split up and addressed as immature or mature. immature meaning unhealthy, unhelpful, toxic behaviors/reasons. mature meaning healthy, helpful, non-toxic behaviors/reasons.

depending on the chapter topic, there will always be a mature/immature* comparison side-by-side to help see at least two potential ways a behavior like why he doesn't communicate (for example) shows up for him. it will look something like this:

the <u>mature</u> lover accepts how what he does impacts you.

he hears you. every word that leaves your mouth.

the <u>immature</u> lover can't be vulnerable.

because he doesn't know what it means.

underlined only here to show difference

a note about repitition: as you read you might say to yourself, "he just said that" or "this feels repetitive" and to be clear, that is intentional. one of the best ways to learn is repetition. just because something is said or done once doesn't mean it is complete, solved, or understood. so if you read passages that overlap, great, you are paying attention.

intended audience: the way hwttbtw is written follows a flow that goes something like this:

1. why he is doing something   2. what you can do about it

'you' in this can literally mean YOU dear reader, about yourself, or what you can do to help/understand 'him' and/or other people.

intended audience (cont.) there may be moments where you might say, "wait, women do this too! why are you singling out men?" and those are valid. but remember, the focus of this book project is to shine light, even if the light is too bright or not bright enough, on why men do certain things. humans, no matter their gender or gender expression have carry over and resemble actions and wants and feelings based on a tremendous amount of things like upbringing, environment, social expectations, stigmas, and so on. so if you find yourself doing that, saying "they do it, too!" cool. then keep reading. keep probing. keep pushing. keep the course. and always ask yourself, *do i do this. are there folks i know who do this. why am i deflecting. how do i feel about this.*

anyone and everyone really interested in the topic of manhood, masculinity, love, and finding critical ways to re-define, re-imagine, re-veal and re-learn what it means to be a man should read this book.

lowercase: sylistic choice since middle school.

outcomes + takeaways: hwttbtw is titled as thesis. as argument. as reason. as call to action. what it isn't is a cop out or stationary. simply leading with *he was taught to be this way.* is a starting point that is totally dependent on what is done after that statement has been made. and saying *he was* *taught to be this way.* for only negative behaviors is misplaced. *he was taught to be this way.* is both and. it is affirming and calling to question. it is intended to underscore totality not just partial fragments. we all have work to do and are responsible for blindspots, brightspots and everything in-between.

he was taught to be this way. has a period at the end not meaning full stop but as a charge. that is to say how can what was taught be unlearned and also how can what was taught be modeled and taught to others to show greater breadth and depth that help and don't hinder. that express and don't deter. that build and don't break. the intention, outcome, and overall takeaway is a request. that if all of us can dig a bit and explore ourselves and commit to even the smallest change, we're all better for it.

gratitude: i need to extend heartfelt gratitude and love for anyone and everyone (named and unnamed) who labored with me on this. whether you read the prototype and gave formal feedback, listened to me talk about my hopes for this project, or gently nudged me to get it done no matter how hard it was, it wouldn't be complete without having had your hearts and words and minds along this journey. thx:
chanel.marley.patti.will.evan.mic.carly.marcus.sarah.hanh. claudia.alexx.mia.reed.dave.justine.6lack.isaac.jaryn.scott. angelica.jmays.tim.project wayfinder.humblethepoet.aaron sr.

a piece for you from me

+++

i'm not even sure if my story
is different from yours
and i try to keep my life
my world my privacy
behind the curtain as much as possible
however
without showing and sharing with you
a flashlight into me
you may not feel the depth of this volume
the weight of this body
so perhaps a few quick lines
can hit your heart
from mine
from this spanish rooftop

really hate to admit this
but talking about my emotions
how i personally feel
makes me uncomfortable
even when i'm in the wrong
even when i've done
foolish things
that hurt the one i love
and i have to check myself
patch myself up

i know i need to change
be another way
too many years
i've swallowed messages
of how to be in this world
of running away
or pretending to be unnerved

maybe that's because
i come from divorce
violent abusive split households
broken love
broken doors
broken vows
broken words
broken bones
and all i could do
and all i had the power to do
was remain silent
was remain quiet
was remain child
was remain observant
was remain complicit
to be seen not heard
product of
traumatic love
so traumatic
my memories
fractured

and i can't ignore my childhood
as it raised me to become
the man that i am today

middle child
big family
perhaps why i accommodate
mediate
try not to create waves
but i have this temper
call it repressed anger
that holidays
that winters
that creeps up
when lessons become too hard to face
when mistakes splinter me from
who i want to be and
who i've been running from
so
when we argue
when we re-visit
old pains
old wounds
old stories
old patterns
i forget to breathe
and revert
to what i was taught
from men before me

the work i have done
just isn't enough
saying sorry
just isn't enough
so
i have to go back
and fetch
all the beautiful
all the terrifying
all the toxic
all the beneficial
teachings said and unsaid
and account for them
lay them bare
and ask myself why
i've collected
uncried tears
and been
a stone wall
to ensure that my son
doesn't inherit
unhealthy practices
and have to atone
for my sins

-- adrian michael
10.6.19 | barcelona, spain

KING

he was taught to be this way.

theking
archetype

he is a king
his soul is royalty
but sometimes his ego
and thirst for power
get the best of him
and his fascination with control
takes hold
choke holds
ability
desire
connectivity
with vulnerability
yet when secure
his words and actions align
the man box fades
steps into what he fears
(his shadow his trauma his inner self)
returning to that poised balanced leader
integrated back to a most humble sovereign
a most genuine loving human being.

he was taught to be this way.

toxicmasculinity
and why he feels superior

toxic masculinity is about power and exerting that power over other men and especially women. weakness by any measure is unacceptable as it goes against what it means to be a man. men can't be emotional or show emotions in public. emotions such as sadness, fear, and shame bumps up against the male bravado.

so rather than give someone the upper hand in the relationship he will do what he can to puff out his chest literally and figuratively.

he feels superior because he was taught to be this way. since birth. before birth even. patriarch society calls for it. begs of it. the lessons are intentional. the lessons are woven seamlessly into the fabric of life. gender roles exploit it. any so-called man that steps out of the system is blasted and ignored if he doesn't fall back in line. systems don't work when the cogs act up. healthy masculinity looks like the awareness and acknowledgment of body, mind, and spirit. how they interact and impact with self and how they interact and impact with others.

toxic masculinity lives in stereotype. reinforces the stereotype. denies and confines a total experience by suppressing the fullness and reality of being human. toxic masculinity also tries to destroy feminine energy that might undermine his manhood. doing anything that remotely looks like it's not boyish or manish and he gets schooled with a jarring three word sentence: *be a man.*

damaging and destructive, these three words are flawed when it lacks variation and nuance. when there are no other times someone says 'be a man' except those that fuel the stereotype then implanted in him is this false sense of maleness. he is given a roadmap that cuts him off from his whole self.

masculinity is a journey into becoming. developing. being. a constant conversation that requires honesty and steadfast commitment to the pursuit of his own definition. his own path to finding if the edges of the "man box" are too sharp and begging to question what courage it will take to call himself from the margin and enter the center where growth happens.

the mature king is emotional.

he isn't afraid to cry.
he isn't afraid to show joy.
he isn't afraid to be affectionate.
he isn't afraid to be vulnerable.
he isn't afraid to admit when he is wrong.
he isn't afraid to share how he's feeling.

the mature king is emotional. his power comes from his ability to access his feelings. the love that he has in his heart isn't hidden and his intentions are always clear. when he wants to download what's going on with him and his world with you he graciously asks if you have the emotional bandwidth to have a deep dialogue and if you aren't he appreciates your honesty. he knows that two souls struggling mindfully together is better than one soul only getting what they need while the other suffers silently.

he overfeels. when you're connected to your heart you must go with the flow. and when in his flow, honoring the king within him, he taps into empathy. sincerely.

the immature king is cold and controlling.

he is controlling and control is a shadow.
it overcompensates for something that is lacking within the man. when it shows up it tries to strip others of their power. makes it so that their voice doesn't matter. call them out. there is an insecurity that is keeping him out of balance.

the immature king doesn't see any relationship that he enters as an equal partnership. each empowered. each having voice. each making decisions. instead he wants to run the show. wants to dictate. wants to rule.
non-emotional, he's not interested in what you feel about his need to control and only believes that being a man means take lead.

when *be a man* means don't withhold your tears
when *be a man* means share how you feel
when *be a man* means ask for permission
when *be a man* means use your words
when *be a man* means her body isn't yours
when *be a man* means think think think
when *be a man* means let go of control
he will begin to see through how cold he's been.

he was taught to be this way.

the mature king is responsible.

he takes principled action to set goals and adjusts accordingly. when setbacks occur the mature king will reflect on the role he played in the situation and problem solves to figure out new ways in which he can achieve something or makes a new plan entirely. he does not blame others.

when given a task he follows through.

his words align with his behaviors.
he is a man of integrity.

the mature king takes relationships seriously. his duty is to himself and to those he loves by honoring commitments, providing loving speech, and ensures that he can take care of any debts he owes. he leaves every space he occupies better than he found it and inspires others to do the same.

that part of a king, that is responsible, humbly takes to task all of these things and more.

the immature king is insecure and expects to be taken care of.

uncertain. always anxious. doubtful. hesitant. unassertive. timid. not firm or confident. the immature king waivers on making decisions on his own and relies heavily on the opinions and advice of others. it is natural to want to make the right choice but he never learned how to be independent.

everything was handed to him. and working hard is out of the question. the immature king is lazy and avoids a challenge. if he comes across someone that pushes him to be better he sabotages the relationship simply by being who he is: inconsiderate. unwilling to compromise. selfish. childish.

he is irresponsible and blames others for mistakes he may of directly caused.

the immature king truly believes he is the center of the universe. everything must revolve around him.

he was taught to be this way.

the mature king isn't intimidated by your success.

in fact, quite the opposite. he builds you up. wants you to reach the greatest heights, even if higher than his own. the mature king knows that if his partner is successful he is successful, and vice versa.

he wouldn't dare bow out of a relationship because your success outshines his. the mature king holds his own and follows his dreams and ambitions while supporting yours. if necessary he would consider pausing what he has going on and pay closer attention to your needs to ensure you are good. he can multi-task but honestly he is a lot better at focusing on a few projects at a time. when his attention is on growing, all things around him will sprout.

if he were to leave you, it wouldn't be because you were more successful. he would leave temporarily to get his matters in order as he may feel like he is undeserving of your love feeling out of balance. he will tell you the truth. he wouldn't quit on you.

the immature king allows his ego to ruin a good thing.

it's hard for a man to admit that he is wrong. his inflated confidence and sense of pride gets in the way of truly seeing what he has in front of him. someone who isn't trying to boast and bruise his ego. but someone who wants to grow with him. someone who is willing to admit their fault not just to move on but to grow and say "my bad".

the immature king allows his ego to ruin a good thing because he was taught to be the breadwinner.

if he is unable to provide for you or his family he feels shame and doesn't know how to cope. he will turn to things to distract him and or become violent or aggressive. he doesn't have the tools to navigate feeling this inadequacy. the immature king, remember, blames others. because he doesn't know how to communicate effectively he will take it out on the easiest targets around him. most times it is on the person he is in a relationship with.

he was taught to be this way.

the mature king makes decisions with you.

it may have taken him awhile to get to this point. maybe he never was in a truly committed long-term relationship before and doesn't know what it looks like. whether he got it right the first time or has stumbled along the way, the mature king knows to make decisions with you.

"me" has become "we" and before anything is final the both of you have weighed the pros, the cons, the what if's and could be's, why's and why nots. he knows if you are not onboard then it isn't worth it. or if you disagree or he disagrees there is an understanding.

together is sometimes better than alone and the mature king knows when to ask for space and undertands when his partner needs their space. choosing to be in a relationship requires shared decision making and respecting one another's independence.

the immature king makes moves when he is ready. not when you are.

recall the piece about control. the immature king thrives and is most comfortable when things are on his terms. if it isn't his idea he more than likely is unwilling to see it through unless he can somehow someway make it about him. he was taught this. he knows no different. think of the child who wants the big wheel bike and adults would rather get him a golf set. what does he do? he whines. he complains. he kicks. he screams. what do they do? they give in. clearly this has happened over the course of his lifetime. kicking and screaming metaphorically until he gets what he wants. or he was the kid that never got what he wanted and saw it displayed by other kids in person or on the laundry list of media outlets (tv, books, movies, etc.) this is no different. he has been practicing this behavior all of his life. or he had been pushed around and has decided to push back. either way, what needs to change is how people respond to it. he needs to know this is not okay.

he was taught to be this way.

thepast
and why he holds on

the past has been written. it is forever gone and there is no going back. it is inked. blotted. printed. the story has run and the replay is archived. the past means old relationships. old flames. old situations. old friends with benefits. old friends that just were friends he never did anything with. old study buddies. old late night chats. old cuddle buddies. old thorns. old ones that got away. old never gave them the time of day. old top 3 friends on myspace. old direct messages on instagram. old penpals. old anything and everything that isn't his present.

it boils down to connection. men might communicate with people from their past because at some point in time they meant something to them. they remind him of good times and being nostalgic or being in direct or indirect communication says what they had is important enough to stay in touch. it can be harmless but with the rise of social media, the lines can be blurred if he intentionally hides it.

comradery is essential to the soul. friendship. love. acceptance. affirmation. human interaction validates existence. and for him, staying connected with people who once saw him. once knew him. once loved him. people he knows who wish nothing but the best for him, affirms his light. whatever they had at the core he felt cared for and is willing to hold on because of their soul tie.

but to him, he may not see what you see. you don't understand this need. you can let go and move on. he is different. this doesn't mean you aren't good enough or the one he will release old bonds for. it means it is that more crucial for you to check in and inquire why he has this need to be friends with people from his past. this will help him. this will tease out a conversation that has probably never happened.

holding on to the past has been an automatic behavior that his head and his heart have normalized for years. don't be surprised if it takes time to unpack or loosen some of his relationships. men sometimes maintain single mindsets while operating in exclusive relationships. he needs to make new connections in his brain. he needs to learn that some people from his past can no longer be in his present. he needs to know why. he needs to make a choice.

the mature king is clear about healthy boundaries.

being direct and up front about his past is hard but he does it to be honest. he could keep things from you and leave you in the dark but the mature king lets you in to make sure there is no doubt about how he feels about you. if he wants to maintain friendships from his past he talks to you about it. surely you will bring up certain discomforts around the relationships he had prior to you. that is normal. he will do everything he can to display respect and understanding of maintaining healthy boundaries.

there are those thorns, people who cause constant irritation in your relationship. no matter what you say or feel or do those thorns take the longest to get out. the mature king recognizes this and even though he no longer has emotional ties to them, he has to let them go. this takes time. some roots run deep.
this doesn't mean he wants them. it means the emotional process must take its course. the mature king tells you from jump so not to catch you off guard.

the immature king hides who he talks to. even if he has nothing to hide.

he does this to fill a void. more than likely he can't name the void or analyze why he does this. humans enjoy some level of attention. and if he is talking to people he shouldn't be or is being secretive about certain interactions, he could be activating that part of him that fills this bucket.

the immature king hides who he talks to because he knows you wouldn't like or understand why he does this. even if it strictly platonic. he could avoid all the hiding if he communicates his need to talk to others but he is unsure as to why he wants to talk to them or is unwilling to be told what he can and can't do. a reason why he maintains connection is because he wants to feel wanted. that he still has "it". he enjoys the rush of new energy offered by someone else. he is doing what he was doing when he was single.

he was taught to be this way.

the mature king lets go of the old. grows with the new.

whoever you fell in love with knows that he will change and become a different version. he will try new things. practice new energies. flow with certain interests that weren't on his rader when you first met. a healthy relationship provides space for this development to happen. it is expected. for everyone.

the mature king sheds his old skin and wants you to grow with him in his new skin. he becomes a better man because he feels loved and has your favor. he knows that his past once held your relationship back and he made the conscious choice to let it go. that old version fades to black.

life requires him to change. not into someone he or others don't recognize. but into his true purpose. when he finds who he is, as ralph ellison says, he will be free. and so too will your relationship. it will ripen and become sweeter. deeper. otherworldly.

the immature king is stuck in his past.

man culture says that you aren't truly a man if you don't get as many girls (women) as possible. like notches on a belt or collecting bottle caps, he is taught to collect women. that this collection is most meaningful because it shows he can pull them. it's a competition. it's a hunt. it's a game. rules dictate that it's just what men do and there are no feelings involved. men go around breaking hearts without consideration. it's live action gaming. except he goes home whole and she goes home torn apart. the immature king is stuck in this disfunctional reality.

he is stuck on who he used to be. how others used to view him. how he used to act. there is a fear to do things differently because it is unexplored territory. he knows no other way. no one around him provided an alternative. if they did, it was too far of a jump. perhaps he is too far gone. in his mind he thinks this way. so why change? why shift? you may not be the one he stays with but be the one that gently reminds him of his true self. if he knew better, he'd be better. sometimes he knows better. he must learn a new language.

he was taught to be this way.

the mature king commits to what he fears.

being alone for an extended amount of time can bring up a lot of anxiety.

so most men who feel anxious around being alone will fill that time in one of two ways: he will notice how he feels and does something that he enjoys that is healthy and positive, constructive like working on a project or exercises or hits up his boys to go and hangout. anxiety can also stem from boredom. when he is bored he doesn't know what to do and as a practice from his single days he will hit up someone and attempt to fill the void with conversation.

the mature king recognizes those patterns of what he does when feeling anxious (boredom) comes up. more than likely he will recall the numerous arguments that were caused by him because of previous things he had done when bored. so he actively works on changing the pattern. his fear evolves and the mature king commits to being alone. his alone time becomes another source of peace where he can work on himself. he trusts himself to be alone. you trust him when he's alone.

the immature king can't be alone.

alone isn't just a physical state but a mental one as well. he can be next to you or be in a room full of people and feel lonely. perhaps he doesn't even want to be there but because he has this deep rooted fear of being alone he would rather surround himself with folk he could care less about over being alone. the immature king uses people for his own interests. be it to release sexual energy or emotional energy once he is satisfied and/or the next best thing comes around he leaves you. from one person to the next the immature king treats people as if they are disposable.

this behavior comes from a wound he still suffers from but never processed. someone hurt or broke his heart and he never recovered. someone left him. someone treated him like he was meaningless and tossed him to the side. and rather than get treated like this again the immature king reclaims a toxic power on his own accord and emotionally detaches himself from potential heartache. he disregards love. doesn't care for it anymore. he is lost to his suffering.

the mature king builds castles with you.

he might not have a castle he calls his own yet. but he has been thinking about it. meditating on it. working towards it. but it isn't just any castle. it's yours. and it's not just one castle. it's many. he has walked this earth long enough to know that he can't just settle down with anyone and that whoever he settles down with can't be a placeholder. they are the real thing. you are the real thing. he will make this known when he is ready. in the beginning, like most relationships, he is feeling you out. getting to know you. seeing where it is going. he may not initiate the "future" talk but he is attentive and listens, feels, and probes your response. as should you.

castles are dreams. castles are investments. castles are children. castles are adventures. castles are homes. castles are your forever. castles are your legacy.

the mature king builds these castles with you.
for you. by you.

the immature king makes you need him.

building a person up takes time. some longer than others. he takes great pride in his ability to use words and sometimes his actions to do this. in this instance the intention isn't honorable. the immature king makes you need him. he pours affirmations that, to you, are true and helpful and necessary and appreciated. but to him, they are only necessary to get you in his cross hairs. for you to think that without him you are nothing. that you can achieve nothing. that you can provide nothing. he builds you up just to break you down. he needs to be needed. in order for that to happen he has to know he has complete control over you. he was taught to provide but this is skewed and distorted in such a way that can be emotionally, physically, spiritually and verbally abusive.

the immature king turns all of his wrongs into your wrongs. makes you feel incapable and the reason for his antics. with you gone he is nothing. his value is determined by the people he maintains. getting you to do what he says when he says it is dominance that he most likely doesn't have in other spaces.

he was taught to be this way.

beingcomfortable
and why you can't leave him

at some point in our life we settle. perhaps we think in that moment it won't get better than what is presented as the option in front of us or we get tired of looking. either way it is a choice. to stop. to refrain from going any further. this choice alters what the following days look like. different from settling down for all the right reasons, this type of settling down is unfulfilling and done for all the wrong reasons. it doesn't sit right. or everyone around us knows something we are unwilling to admit to ourselves.

there are good men. there are bad men. and any man can cross onto both sides. no man is perfect. both will tell you and show you who they are.

despite popular belief that men are simpletons, they are complex and deep and misunderstood because there is no universal handbook on how to navigate a healthy relationship. the relationships they did see may have been saturated in traditonal gender roles or the men in their life were always with a different woman or there were no men in their tribe that sat down and explicitly talked about how to treat someone you romantically love.

learning by consumption (watching and listening) is absorbed into the pysche with little to no thinking. it becomes imprinted and soon imitated. imagine if he sees a man in his life put hands on a woman. if he doesn't have someone tell him that that behavior is not okay then he will assume that it is normal and acceptable and eventually may find himself in a situation he will regret. putting your hands on anyone without their consent is never okay. this is a boundary he may never have learned.

buying flowers. being affectionate. opening doors. buying dinner. walking them home. writing notes. not raising your voice. and other types of examples may have never been consumed. it has to be taught.

some men convince you that all that romantic stuff is unnecessary and that he shows love in different ways but at the core it taps into a softer side that he was never allowed to explore. rather than experiencing that discomfort he blatantly disregards it and deflates that part of himself. one way you both settle is by over time being okay with not getting what you want.

the mature king settles down for the right reasons.

he loves you. you complete him. he's happy. he's not holding your heart hostage. his future has you in it.

he has met his equal.
he lets it be known. family. friends. universe.
he is ready for forever. with you. and only you.

all that he values is embodied in you. he sees it. he honors it. he cherishes it. and when the time is right the mature king settles down. this happens when he decides to let go of everything that was holding him back from true commitment.

not just anyone gets his attention. the mature king sees beyond the exterior of a person and focuses on the interior. what's inside the soul. the inauthentic ones quickly go. when the mature king feels no pressure, can be his authentic self, and is soul tied to his chosen mate he is locked in. he waited long enough to meet the one.

the immature king guilt trips you from leaving.

he can't be alone. remember? maybe he has shared some of his story with you. maybe he has kept most of it to himself. but he does know when to use his past against you. whether you are serious or not even mentioning plans to get out of the relationship brings up the "oh, so you gonna leave just like the rest of them huh?" comment. and it hits you. maybe it's news to you and those words feel like (to you) that he is opening up and really doesn't want you to go. the immature king guilt trips you. he might really want you to stay and he might just not want to be alone. you know the guy. right? either way this tactic is another form of control. trying to make you feel bad for his behavior. his wrongs. his choices. rather than own his stuff (be accountable) it is easier for the immature king to play victim. amateur reverse psychology may even convince you that you can't leave because by leaving you would have wasted all the time you have accrued with him. the trap is set..

the mature king knows you are royalty, too.

he's the kind of king that knows his crown isn't on his head but in his soul. king is a state of mind. state of heart. state of hand. he sees the royalty in you. he doesn't compare or judge or belittle or patronize or abuse or lead on or play or deny or control you. the mature king sees the divine in you. he honors all that you are. all that you accomplish. all that you aspire. all that you create. all that you are becoming.

he knows
you are water
powerful enough to drown him
soft enough to cleanse him
deep enough to save him

you are the kind of royalty
that knows your crown
isn't on your head
but in your soul

you are magic. the mature king knows this truth.

the immature king stays immature. he doesn't want to grow.

and he definitely doesn't want to support your growth. by you improving and setting higher heights in sight it causes him to reflect on his life and what he wants. because he doesn't like change and set in his ways he rejects the new you. or the you that wants to see you both develop internally. you want to connect spiritually. go deeper. explore other avenues of your relationship but the immature king stays immature. he is stunted. can't see beyond who he currently is. he thinks you are trying to change him, that you don't like who he currently is. but your love is at the horizon and he is only looking at the waves at his feet. the discomfort of being uncomfortable thinking of doing something he hasn't done like going to a wellness workshop or an adventure you've always wanted to try, block him from insights that can add to his world, not take away. the immature king would rather stay in the world he has already created. and that is too bad because the world you want to create with him is better. doing things together is always beautiful.

WARRIOR

thewarrior
archetype

protective he must be
holding the weight of
what the world expects
and balancing what his
soul requires. the walls
he defends. the gateke-
eper must decide when
to go to battle and how
to retreat when a flood
of emotions grounds
him. the war in him
is a fight he won't win
unless he finds a way
to make peace with
all that buried pain.

he was taught to be this way.

protective
and why he will or won't fight for you

different from control, in a healthy situation,
a man vows to his loved one that no harm will
come to them so long as he is concerned. this
pledge is a chivalrous act. a call to action.
a promise. a responsibility.

he holds himself to the same standard. he too must
follow this commandment of not just protecting you
from outsiders, but protecting you from him as well.
he will always do his best to ensure that he isn't the
cause of your pain or your tears.

when he truly cares about you it is instinctive. the
protector in him unleashes. if you are walking by a
road and the cars are driving on your side he will
make sure that he is closest to the road. instinct.
care. he would see harm come to him first before it
ever were to reach you. it is his duty. he protects.
he stands up for you if someone tries to assault your
character. he corrects them if they try to disrespect
you in any way. and he steps in if they try to holler

at you. he is yours. not in a bad way. for you are his. a protective male will walk you to your car whether in broad daylight or on the darkest night. it makes no difference. both provide him more time to be with you. both provide him time to show he cares for you. this is one less thing for him to worry about. one less thing for you to worry about. if he is unwilling to walk you, unwilling to hold the door, unwilling to be between you and traffic, unwilling to claim you as his, he is definitely not going to fight for you when the relationship gets hard.

those minute examples may seem base or old school but they are indicators to consider. if he is unwilling to do these small considerate things more times than not he will be too lazy to do anything if what the two of you have is going down hill. he won't check in on you to see why you were short with him or why you were crying or why you hung up the phone or why you no longer look at him the same or why you haven't seen one another in days. this man isn't protective. this man is inconsiderate. not interested. clueless. childish.

but if he is smart he knows that you are precious. treasure. heavenly. magic. and won't allow your love to break down. and if it does, he does anything and everything to protect what you have.

he was taught to be this way.

the mature warrior is mindful.

he has conquered the ability to be aware of himself and others. although it is always easier to be dismissive, he knows that it is his responsibility to breathe and pause and even request space to collect his thoughts before engaging in an uncomfortable hard heated discussion.

the mature warrior is mindful of when he is guarded and comes off as defensive. he apologizes and clarifies what is going on and tells you what he needs.

he picks his battles strategically and doesn't allow himself to get triggered by everything. the mature warrior recognizes that his energy is sacred and knows that he is the attention that he gives. that people appreciate his words. his thoughts. his advice. his presence. so he chooses them wisely. the mature warrior is not cocky. he is confident. he stands firm in his values and is willing to revisit those values if they impact others negatively.

when he is with you he is yours. he wants to know you. all of you. what sets your soul on fire. what passions you. what keeps you up at night. he connects deeply.

the immature warrior is defensive.

always on guard, the immature warrior gets triggered by the most trivial of things. questions that are directed at him feel like attacks and to protect himself he sends a flare of aggression to dead the conversation. whether avoiding being honest or just doesn't want to talk, he feels as if you are being intrusive and that part of him that doesn't fully trust, inquisitions your intentions. he may be paranoid that you are only asking to set him up, catch him in a lie, or get all up in his business. even if you are the love of his life, he values privacy but doesn't know how to verbalize it without it coming off as secretive. one of the biggest reasons he's defensive is because he doesn't know how to navigate his feelings. whether sad, ashamed, afraid, or angry he was taught to never show it in public. so checking on him in a moment where one or more of this emotions presents itself he can't own what is going on. he responds the only way he has practiced. by being defensive. by blocking. by leaving. by dismissing. the immature warrior is really good at ridding himself of emotions. even happiness becomes void. he's serious. too serious. his walls are high. his guard is up.

the mature warrior is loyal.

he puts his needs well below the needs of others. he commits himself to the craft of love and service to the loves of his life. the mature warrior's loyalty runs deep. he is faithful to all things he sets his heart, mind, and soul upon. his unwavering desire to see you happy is his cause. his appetite. his longing. he notices when your days are long and you're too tired to complete the next task. he genuinely does what he can to take any weight off your shoulders and chest so you can rest.

the mature warrior journeys to vibe with you on a spiritual level. whether you believe in energy, spirits, god, the universe, humanity, or anything in-between he is interested in learning and loving you. that is what relationships are all about: people willing to consider the thoughts and practices of others with care and respect with the understanding that there is room to disagree and argue in order to grow.

he is your champion. your cheerleader. your servant. your knight. your advocate. your rock. your ride-or-die. your soldier. your man. he will never abandon you.

the immature warrior is selfish.

he seeks after personal gain and glory. he doesn't care how many hearts he has bulldozed. his compassion for you is limited because he can't see outside of himself.

love is always a good cause. it is liberating. beautiful. giving. unselfish. the immature warrior isn't interested in that. love, to him, is sport. a game. a conquering match. a battle to always have the upper hand. he doesn't want a title. he doesn't want to name whatever it is the two of you have going on. titles confine the immature warrior because he feels attached to a cause. to a person. to a war that he can't easily get out of. not being officially attached allows him to slip in and out undetected. he prefers being in multiple battles where he is victor rather than just one where he might be victim.

the immature warrior sees that he is capable to feel. to fall. to love. but vulnerability is his kryptonite. he becomes powerless and controlling his emotions by locking them away is function of his selfishness. with his guard up there is no getting through.

he was taught to be this way.

the mature warrior knows you are strong.

and he knows you don't need saving.

in fact, he stays in your gravitational pull. your galaxy. your energy. your love. because of this. your strength attracts him. there is something about a woman who stands in her confidence and doesn't dim her light. the mature warrior doesn't want a damsel. he wants another warrior. he is secure in how mighty, how powerful, how independent you are. the mature warrior knows that tears are a sign of fortitude and not weakness. seeing this side of you gives him permission to lay at the edge of your well and help pull out more water. to go deeper. to navigate with you. he is unafraid of your feelings because they remind him to feel. to go inside of himself. to find that inner strength that you so gracefully model for him. and if you struggle sourcing your water, he gently takes his caring soul down there with you. and sits in the darkness for as long as it might take. you are stronger together.

he loves that you are a knight polishing your armour. carrying your own sword. fighting your own battles. making your own glory.

the immature warrior doesn't listen.

he is programmed to be really good at tuning you out. as you talk. as you share. as you invest. as you unfold. as you fight. as you queen. he is wandering. his mind is elsewhere. he has mastered the ability to make you think that he is listening. paying attention. focusing. on you. your words. your heart. but no. not much goes through his ears unless it's about him. his survival. his path.

the immature warrior cannot multi-task. things have to be done one at a time. stretching himself to cater to you and to himself he will ensure that his needs are met first. always. he can't be hungry while feeding you.

don't get your hopes up. you can't train him or force him or be patient enough for this to change. the immature warrior will emphatically tell you that he is stuck in his ways and that he has been this way all of his life. he believes that he is stone. even if you were to trickle your water on his hard exterior and somehow bore a hole, he will complain and tell you that he changed because of you. this will not last unless he chooses to change for himself. tread lightly, beautiful.

he was taught to be this way.

suffering
and how he copes with pain

the man who suffers turns his pain into different forms of power. he will use it as a means to avoid other people having to deal with what he has gone through or he will go out of his way to put people through worse fires. suffering in any capacity is hard. harsh. difficult. but how man works through it. responds to it. engages with it. is what matters.
it sets him apart.

if he has been burnt in the past and hasn't processed those situations he internalizes. he retreats. he falls inside himself. he does no soul work. instead he suffers outwardly but doesn't know it. he suffers inwardly but doesn't know it. how it shows up. how his pain peaks is how he treats you. how he refuses to get close. how he views you as an object. how he goes through one after another after another after another. he becomes soul dangerous. not only is he damaging everyone, he is damaging himself.

when you get frustrated and mad and wonder why

he's so distant. so unavailable. so uninterested. he gets pleasure by seeing you go through pain. this is in his control. being detached from his emotions gives him the upper hand that wasn't at his disposal in past relationships. so here he is, retaliating. his words aren't soft. his actions are cold. this man will do nothing to soothe you. he's dismissive because his guard is up. his walls are high. he is fortified. he may have even told himself to never open up again.

this will go on until someone, maybe you, calls him out. encourages him to take a look at himself. if he is too far gone he must seek professional help to give him practical tools and strategies to talk about his hurt. his disconnect. his issues. it's not your responsibility to be his savior. more than likely he won't listen to you anyway. men prefer to suffer alone. to fix himself. but when he becomes reflective and recognizes the trail of tears he has left behind, he will stop blaming others. he will say enough is enough. he will do what has to be done.

a self-aware man knows that suffering is a choice. he will authentically expose himself to you by sharing some of the battles he is facing. he will ask you to be his mirror. to be honest when some of his darkness creeps up on him.

he was taught to be this way.

the mature warrior moves on.

he doesn't hold grudges. the mature warrior knows that he can do nothing about his past except for move on and learn from those he gave his heart to. rather than hold disdain, he understands that it takes a lot more energy to hate someone than it does to let go and forgive. this doesn't mean that he forgets but he is careful to ensure that he drills down what role he played in the downward spirals and what role they played. he analyzes the difference and owns his contribution.

the mature warrior tells you his story while it is being written. he used to keep his failures to himself but he knows that in order for there to be a future with you he will courageously invite you into the fire. keeping what attaches him is what got him in trouble with others, so to not repeat past offenses he is upright and open. maybe to a fault, he might overshare. but at least he lets you in by telling you what he is working on and how you can support him. if it is too much for you to handle, he will thank you. he will honor you. he will bow out gracefully and continue working on himself.

the immature warrior holds on. revenge fuels his appetite.

maybe he doesn't want to see you happy or with someone else. maybe he finds parts of you in other people. maybe he tries so hard to get you back. whatever he does he obviously is stuck. the immature warrior won't let go or admit defeat because it isn't over unless he says so. this is destructive and tyrannical.

sometimes he can't differentiate between perception and reality. the world is at his beck and call. he can do no wrong. he can pinpoint all the words. thoughts. actions. inactions. disfunction. in others towards him but those same things he is blinded to when he does it to them. he is out of touch. his tantrums have pushed people who care about him away. in his mind you left because you don't love him. he has abandonment issues. he gets you back by making you feel worthless. like he only gave you the time of day because he felt sorry for you. because no one else wanted you and that he felt it was his duty to cover you. the immature warrior is wounded. revenge fuels his appetite.

the mature warrior is decisive.

he gets tired of hearing the same thing over and over and not doing anything about it. he no longer wants to take out his aggression towards you. it eats at him. for he knows the toll it takes. the mature warrior decides to create big goals. one of those goals is to rid himself of what torments him and continuously visits him in relationships. he writes it down to make it real. for far too long he avoided the truth. but he is different now. not to be confused with perfect. he is far from that. one of those goals is not to be perfect, but to be different. to seperate himself from the version that broke hearts. that didn't see the tremendous value in you. he decides to make amends. the insults. the injuries. the losses. the mature warrior doesn't pardon himself. he vows to keep you safe from the return of the old him.

another one of his goals is deciding to choose you over choosing himself. he has practiced choosing himself and you see where that has gotten him. so this is new for him. but he is committed to building a new life. with you. for you. for him.

the immature warrior torments you because he's in pain.

at least that's what he makes you think.

he has no self control. he even knows that he treats you like crap because of his weathered past. but his self awareness is only lip service. he does nothing about it.

the immature warrior would have you believe that his failures with you are because he is operating in wounds but that is half truth. if he were fully true he would fess up to the fact that he enjoys tormenting you because he himself enjoys his own pain. hurting you fills him. this sadistic ritual is a trap. a vicious whirlwind that he keeps you in. how it works? boy meets girl. boy loses girl. boy sucks her back in by lying that he will change. boy gets girl back. boy hurts girl again. boy makes her feel like it was her fault. girl feels bad. girl stays. boy hurts her again. boy blames girl. cycle repeats. a cautionary tale.

the mature warrior aligns with you. he doesn't fight you.

imagine what a partnership looks like. a real one. not something that is one-sided or based off of intimidation or force. it must be genuine and entered into with no expectation to get anything in return except for honesty. love. respect. and friendship. that is basic. for him, the mature warrior seeks an ally who will join forces. to partner and defend one another. to keep their relationship sacred and private. to not allow outside commentary, outside influence, or outside distractions penetrate and break them down.

the mature warrior aligns with you. your dreams. your happiness. your everything. it makes him better. it gives him further purpose. he thrives off of knowing he is in your life. that no one else in this world shares the bond that you two share. he is not threatened by other people in your life. he is well aware that your partnership works because before you came together you were two independent souls. flourishing. still you are two lives. two heartbeats. he trusts you. he doesn't fight you.

the immature warrior avoids mirrors. he's scared of reflection.

he can't stand to be called out. he can do no wrong. in this obscured state of being, the immature warrior avoids mirrors. people who serve as light bearers and guideposts. because they make him uncomfortable. he isn't accustomed to the practice of scrutiny. told that what he's doing is wrong. or how to improve. he surrounds himself with yes people. folk who don't project or pass judgment. folk who go along just to get along. they too are in a mirrorless world. for if they could see the bigger picture, see the root of their own doings, even have deeper conversations about their inner selves, they would be sharper. upstanding. kind and gentle. but they are far from that.

the immature warrior doesn't recognize the person if glass were placed in front of him. he asks who this person is and why he is being shown. he's dismissive and short. unsettled and removed. he doesn't see the point. he is scared of his reflection. mirrors are proof. hard evidence. conclusive. raw. he flees from truth.

he was taught to be this way.

ego
and why he's so good at russian roulette

men have a tendency to not back down even if in the wrong because the ego is so strong. if he is unable to check his ego when it shows up, it can be like playing russian roulette: it's either going to be him or it's going to be you. his ego is the loaded gun. you have no idea when it is going to go off. his pride is at stake and pride is monumental for him.

the unchecked ego gives an inflated sense of pride, and when he feels tested to prove that he is better, tougher, manlier, there is no level of de-escalation practice in reach that will ground him. the wrong kind of guidance pointed him in the direction that confused pride with arrogance and led him on the path to believe that its him against the world. that man is meant to take what it is and not to worry about who gets left behind or negatively impacted. manhood was being modeled by those who were robbed of an official and necesarry rites of passage. the transition from boy to man is being steered by immature and underdeveloped spirits with no vision or understanding of ritual. of process. of responsibility. of legacy. of growth. manhood teachings have been stripped and replaced with empty meaning. baseless lessons. the problem is that too many so-called men are interested in controlling and dictating the training, the raising, the guiding. the problem is that not enough are in it for duty. too many are in it for the position. the power. the misdirection is the result. ego needs ego to continue this cycle. men aren't teaching boys to become men. boys are teaching boys to be pseudo-men. the non-knowing making things up as they go leading the unknowingly to soon do the same for those that come after.

setting his ego aside means he doesn't know. that he is willing to admit that he doesn't know. it takes courage to yield to ego. to rise against it and forfeit its grip takes less energy than it does to keep it at the helm. wanting to be right. wanting to be at the center of every decision. needing to be right. all the time. consumes him. keeps him away from experiencing himself and things outside his self.

ego gets him trouble. causes turmoil. creates a narrative that barriers him further and further away from people. the story he tells himself is that no one understands but in reality, he doesn't realize he shows up all about him. never making enough space for others to share. to speak. to grow. to breathe.

he was taught to be this way.

the mature warrior knows what biases he has about women.

he knows all the stereotypes and what society deems as gender roles. he's even aware of the biases he has and other widely held stories that he is actively working towards re-writing or at least noticing. the mature warrior does what is in his power to change the narrative in his own world and within his spere of influence because he knows that he came from a woman. that his daughters came from a woman. that his sisters and neices and other incredible women were born from a woman. he knows first hand all the ways systems are set up to put men on a higher level. and for what? to maintain that power structure. a man knows not the pain of labor and delivery so it is easier for him to seperate himself from the weight women have to carry. some men will start caring as soon as the baby comes but the mature warrior steps in the moment it is revealed that she is carrying.

he is a product of his environment. so do not blame him outright. give him a chance to unlearn and re-learn. the mature warrior does all of this on his own.

the immature warrior is a male chauvinist.

as defined, a male chauvinist denigrates women under the belief that they are inferior to men. therefore deserving of less than equal treatment. the immature warrior blindly steps into this despicable framework. his words. his actions. his feelings. his entire being buys into this and he is too indoctrinated to see his way out. he passes the torch of male superiority to his sons and makes his daughters drink from the same muddied waters. he makes his entire household, his entire network, his entire presence, sick with these notions.

the immature warrior will dig his heels. clench his fists. turn into a blazing hot sun. to defend his stance. he will say things like "that's just the way it is" and "you knew this about me when we met" or "this is me. i can't change" or "this is a man's world." this immature attitude fuels him. falsely provides him a leg up. when in reality he is simply insecure and afraid of the magic of a woman.

because he was taught that he was better than and to "never get beat by a girl" he has a hard time when he sees them lightyears ahead of him. he is lost.

he was taught to be this way.

the mature warrior has a balanced ego. he is respectful and protects yours.

he knows that you have an ego too. that is where self worth. sense of self. and confidence come from. he is mindful when he feels his ego rise. he senses when yours rises too. he doesn't become combative or resistant. he doesn't feel challenged or have any desire to assert so-called authority. he is level. balanced. secure. will stand his ground for he won't be walked over. as you wouldn't be walked over. the warrior in him is able to scan every situation and clearly resolve, address, and negotiate it without his ego being bruised. this is no easy task. this is an art. for he will want to raise his voice and get his point across if he feels misunderstood. but he doesn't. he takes a cool breath. pauses. tames the fire that tempts to grimace.

the mature warrior will fight for you. not as savior. you can fight for yourself. but as sincere ally. back-up when you need. sometimes two egos are better than one.

the immature warrior has low self-esteem.

his attitude towards himself depends on the people he surrounds himself with. if he saturates himself with people that disrespect others. aren't goal oriented. angry all the time. have control issues. get into trouble constantly. only value material things. could care less about anything meaningful... it seeps inside him. he is a product of who he chooses to expose himself to. the immature warrior has low self-esteem because if he were to evaluate his circle, he'd see what you see.

he would pull himself from under negative energy and fill himself with positive energy. in turn impacting every relationship. but due to his outlook on life (entitled to be given everything. doesn't want to work hard. he should be catered to. long-term plans are non-existent) the immature warrior is stuck. by staying in this lifestyle he more than likely is sad. even depressed. and he takes it out on you. for how he treats you is simply a projection of how he sees and feels about himself. there is hope. he can shift. he can grow. he can rise. he can emerge from this funk. ask him what he wants. ask him where he wants to be. ask him how you can support him. ask him how he wants you to love him.

the mature warrior knows when to end the fight. knows when to surrender.

"why do we love someone so much even when we know we are never meant to be with each other?"

humans are drawn to one another in ways that can't always be explained. and the practice of pinpointing the science of love dictates that we seek reason. to define. to understand. sometimes we get in the way of genuine connection and ruin what could have been. or talk ourselves out of why we can never be. the mature warrior is aware of this and can see the difference between establishing a necessary boundary, notices when others put them up, and observes the dynamic that's brewing. this also speaks to a relationship that may never see longevity - he knows when to end what doesn't feel right - when to step away from an unwinnable fight - when to surrender to a love that was never meant to be. the mature warrior can also sense a friendship that oversteps its bounds in the event it bumps up against his loving relationship with his partner. his spouse. his lover.

the immature warrior won't fight for you. he doesn't deserve your heart.

"why do we continue to fight for someone that may not even deserve our heart?"

you would fight for someone you really wanted. wouldn't you? but how can you fight for someone when they don't show up to the battle field? they don't show up to the conversation? aren't interested in listening to the problems you are having? unwilling to hear how their behavior is impacting you? you can't. you are only fighting yourself while the immature warrior claims to be too busy doing other things. he may even mind trick you into believing it's all in your head and that you are the problem. not him. he doesn't deserve your heart. but he might once you leave but don't do that as a means to get him to fight. he will lure you back in and continue to be how he always was. the idea of him is greater than the credit you give him. he won't fight for what he doesn't want. he lost a good thing the moment he stopped trying.

MAGICIAN

themagician
archetype

he
can
alchemist
make
magic
turn
hearts
into
gold
or
be
trickster
play
games
break
hearts
ruin
souls

he was taught to be this way.

playinggames
and why the fog keeps him from growing up

fog gets in the way. you can't clearly see. when his eyes adjust to this tinted cloud he knows no different. it becomes a natural prescription. not only does his vision become cloudy he breathes it in and his body becomes addicted to it. this fog is the treatment of women. the mistreatment. the division. the caste. the laws. the policies. the unwritten. the de facto. he is raised in it. taught how to power through. to not question. to play the game. to never get played.

in turn each man becomes a walking haze. the physical embodiment that has absorbed the toxins that maintain the imbalance. most, when told about this, will think you're crazy. they don't see what you see. they are inside. reaping the benefits of things tilted in his favor. unwilling to investigate a mythical fog. he's accustomed to ordering his steps so stepping outside this world never crosses his mind. he never has to think about the safety of his own body. it is a given that nothing will be done to him unless he approves it. in his world he is the offense. he is the defense. he is the referee. he is the point system. he is the coach. and you... you are the ball.

when you get flat. he blames you.
when you don't hit the target. he blames you.
when you go out of bounds. he blames you.
when you get lost. he blames you.
when you get old. he finds another you.

the fog convinces him that everyone is bound by the same rules and until his body is under fire, under attack, infringed upon, he will never understand #metoo or truly get rid of the vermin that pillage the bodies of women for sport. because to him, what's the big deal? men trapped in the fog are those that see what is happening around them as normal.

warfare on the bodies of women has been normalized, ritualized, and passed down. like a willed inheritance. and he who inherits rarely gets the history of where things came.

but he has the power to unplug. to escape. to push back. to question. to change. to challenge men who feel entitled to her body. and it can't take womankind to be his teacher. he can't wait for a woman close to him to be hurt before he can see how he is part of the problem.

the mature magician is an alchemist.

he uses his charisma in a loving and non-misleading way to attract, charm and influence you. just by being him, he compels you. the mature magician is an alchemist. when his spirit comes into contact with yours it's as if he grabs you by the heartstrings and you're hooked. how is this possible? he doesn't intentionally say, "i want you so i will do anything to get you." no. he keeps working on himself. he reads. he writes. he creates. he plans. he grows. he isn't perfect but he is training himself in the art of self love. to be his own sun before shining on someone else. to seek success in the ways of taking care and acknowledging blind spots.

his philosophy isn't for everyone but he knows that if and when he lets you in, you will help make him better. hand in hand, you become gold.

whether you both are dealing with hardship, or either of you one at a time, he puts his magic on you. slowly at first, then all at once. the mature magician doesn't take love lightly. he knows its power. its pull. its spell. he uses it to heal.

the immature magician is a player.

a trickster. a gambler. a hustler. an illusionist. he subscribes to a character outside of himself. he deploys his "good guy" facade and plays up to everything you would ever want him to be. deep down he is those things: nice. chivalrous. respectful. someone you would want to meet the parents. but he is deeply latched to a matrix. to a game. to a world riddled in a fog that he can't get out of. his crew is immersed in it. his influences posture and exploit it. the system recycles it.

with you he is present. for a while. the fog follows him. no escaping its pull. the force of it eventually seduces him to syphon his attention towards another. and another. and another. perhaps you notice his lack of presence in such a way that if he is there with you he really isn't there. his desire to chill with you as much may dimenish. his affection. his words. his all. may dwindle because he has gotten what he wanted. the immature magician is a player. he succumbs to the fog. it can be subtle or it can be overt but he never stays. he can't. he doesn't know how. when the fun fades so does he.

the mature magician inspires you.

by being himself and showing you who he is and what his layers look like, he lets you occupy spaces not just anyone is permitted to enter. just like you, he knows that his home is sacred. this isn't selfish. it is necessary.

for without concern of who recieves his energy he can become scattered and have no part to call his own. you see this and wonder how he does it without coming off as boujee or exclusive. his humility provides a mystery to be unlocked. the mature magician inspires you in such a way that you don't know it is actually happening. you begin to analyze your circles. your decisions. your life. for the better. he doesn't directly ask you to change. he influences you just by being around him. and vice versa. he believes that iron sharpens iron. that even the sharpest blade cannot cut itself. he may not always have the clarity that he needs but when things are unclear there is a calm purpose that overcomes him. he looks for answers. he doesn't ignore the lessons that come out of each situation. easy for him to maneuver around challenge but he prefers to face it. head on. no matter how hard. because he is better for it. he has run away from his problems far too many times.

the immature magician keeps you a secret.

keeping you on the low. in low light. discrete. allows him to keep his single status. allows him to navigate other low light, secretive, in the dark, relationships. for fear of losing a good one, he won't be upfront and tell you that he would like to see other people. or he doesn't want the others to know that he is kicking it with you. covering his tracks the immature magician operates this way because you let him. this is not passing the blame off. this is his excuse. because ya'll haven't defined what you are or he has pleaded to just be friends who get to act like lovers in a non-committed arrangement without strings attached.

he doesn't bring you above ground or claim you. this foundation already blocks future growth. future potential. ever meet up at a public place and he doesn't acknowledge you but if either of you leave he will send you a text like, "it was good seeing you. what are you doing later?" this is problematic. he gets away with it. this isn't going where you want it to go.

the mature magician makes you feel like buried treasure.

you are special. he knows this. you know this. but he reminds you often. when you least expect it. we all get down on ourselves and he notices when you slip into feeling a certain way. his mission is to uncover every bit of buried treasure inside and outside of you. things you may have forgotten about. things you didn't know were even there. the mature magician makes any blemish feel like beautiful magic. he turns a simple compliment into poetic soliloquy. words you tell yourself he somehow helps keep afloat.

this isn't about being rescued or raising you out of despair. he wholespiritedly climbs. soars. dives. wades. sits. digs. plants. waters. honors. cares...because of you. he knows that your happiness is linked. whether friend or lover there is a kindness about him that attracts you and keeps you in his atmosphere. as he brings to light the light you contain within, he has no motive to take advantage but rather be another lighthouse to keep yours on and remind you that every part of you is great.

the immature magician leads you on.

he doesn't want a relationship. he knows this all along but he thinks you're cute. thinks you're cool to be around. just not cool enough to stick around. he listens to you talk about what kind of guy you need. the kind of guy you deserve. he takes note. he can be all of that and more. but because he has already resigned himself to be friends with benefits he isn't looking at you with future in his eyes. he is interested in the here and now. and how he can get close to you. he only needs you temporarily. either he just got out of a situation that he wishes he was still in or he jumped from another companion like he typically does. either way, his timing is on his terms. and he is counting down.

the immature magician is leading you on. without consulting you he is making choices for you by lying to you. you see this going somewhere. he sees it going nowhere. but he makes you feel incredible. beautiful. the only one. special. when in actuality you're sadly just a pit stop. a short holiday. he was gone before he came.

he was taught to be this way.

the mature magician doesn't catch just to release.

he is patient. methodical. sometimes confusing. this confusion comes only because you can't see where his head is at times. he is casing you. he is wondering. he is observing. he is planning his steps in real-time. and this behavior frustrates you. of course it does. yet this kind of frustration isn't born out of the desire to know his intentions (he has already told you he isn't into games). your frustration is rooted in wanting the landscape to be articulated. you want him to paint what he sees with your skin as the palette. and he will. he already has. the mature magician honors your sunshine and doesn't like losing light. so he basks in it as much as he can without even talking at times. he doesn't like ruining moments with words. this doesn't mean he is quiet or shy or passive. it means he knows the power of silence. the power of the moment. the power of you.

the mature magician does not lure. he does not tease. he does not dabble. he is an all-in gentle man who doesn't catch just to release. if you end up with him
you'll be safe and in good hands.

the immature magician lures you in just to see if you'll let him in.

and it has become an addiction. a cruel habit. something he does to entertain himself. it's mechanical. and no one is off limits. he may find you through mutual friends or on the instagram explore page. depending on his interests and who he hangs around he will approach you unexpectedly. and you will be taken off guard. perhaps flattered. but wonder what his motives are. as you should. but he won't let you in on his mission. his tour. his one-sided rendezvous.

he will make nice. befriend you. gather personal information from you. get to know you. want to get inside your world. he will begin to push the envelope to see if you're interested. dropping hints here and there to see if you bite. he wants to feel loved. wants to feel wanted. wants to know that he still got it. and you like the attention. even start looking forward to talking to him. then he disappears.

he was taught to be this way.

cheating
and why relationships feel like doing hard time

relationships, whether in or out of marriage, have shifted. the purpose, at its root, has remained the same but the function and longevity of them are different depending on the couple. historically, marriage was an arrangement. a business deal. a display. some, to this day, remain as such. presentations. displays for society. for acceptance. for status. the illusion can fool people outside the bonds of vows or agreements but at some point those inside must determine if they are operating in a transaction or if they are watering one another with love.

he may have a hard time with this if he entered the relationship on false premises. if he didn't do it 100% willingly. it is admirable to not want to hurt someone but honesty up front saves a thousand lost nights of tears. when the hailing advice from men to men about marriage is "life will no longer be the same" or reference to your significant other as the "old ball and chain" it's toxic messaging. it diminishes the divine with playful jest but underneath the damaging wordplay are hints of code that seep inside him. for some it never gets triggered. for others it jolts. it latches. he forgets his wedding ring. his loyalty to the game is stronger than his loyalty to his mate.

you are more than enough and he knows that. and yet some part of him isn't fulfilled. you can't do anything about it. it is up to him to find a way to fill that void. fill that emptiness. fill what he feels is incomplete. but first he must be self-aware. he must be strong enough to look inside himself and do some soul work. some soul searching. he may not like what he discovers but rather than look outside his relationship he must look within it. but some men would rather make you believe everything is okay rather than be vulnerable enough to let you in and be honest about what he is struggling with. if he knew better, he would know that there is incredible strength in exposing that side of him he rarely lets others see. he must learn to be open. to crumble.

he cheats because he is unhappy. he is scared. he is sad. he is ashamed of the vault he has created. rather than examine what he is dealing with, he expresses what he bottles up by emotionally and or physically disconnecting from his mate. some may not see this as a big deal but cheat culture is poisonous.

the mature magician invests his energy on you.

one of his better qualities is that he knows how to be attentive. he is well versed in your love language and when he feels or is told that he's been emotionally recluse or distant he responds. better yet, because he is thoughtful he rarely needs to be reminded. the mature magician invests his energy on you. and when he does that, he is connected. he is attuned. if the vibe seems to be off, even if slightly, he adjusts. makes time to fill you. to whole you. to whole himself. even if that means stopping what he is doing to inhale you. gift you. affirm you. touch you. visit you. serve you.

he knows what gives you butterflies.

there is a part of him that activates when you are around. you both feel it. it is unconscious and lovely. the mature magician ensures to cultivate this. watering you is therapeutic. the breath you provide him is most beautiful magic. the breath that he provides you is the most refreshing air. an oxygen only for you.

the immature magician is dishonest.

a relationship without honesty is a boat without paddles. it isn't going anywhere. it may float. it may stay above water. it may even go further than you'd expect it to. but with no direction and no mechanism to steer it, it is lost at sea. capsize on the horizon. the immature magician isn't good at being truthful. he is really a master of deception because lying or withholding key information is a way to tell you what he thinks you want to hear. you are fully equipped and willing to be upfront. ready to be honest. and when he tells you all the right things. all the beautiful colorful words. you believe him. why wouldn't you. if you catch him in a lie, his lies have lies. his excuses have excuses. his motive is to not be emotionally attached. dishonesty is his problem and potion.

the immature magician just doesn't want any trouble. doesn't want to get in trouble or cause trouble so any question you ask, his first line of defense (because he feels under attack) is to deflect and lie. this is his way of protecting himself. even if he has done nothing wrong. telling the truth has burned him too many times. he must know you aren't trying to trap him.

the mature magician knows you're infinity times enough.

just thinking about you pushes him to think of other ways to show how much he adores you. he doesn't like when you get down on yourself when the pressure to conform and look like societal norms gets the better of you. insecures you. he loves you just the way you are. and when he tells you. believe him. his actions lift you in such a way that your enough is so damn plentiful he sees how you inspire others. your enough is the kind that gifts him peace. he's not looking or feening or wishing or hoping or vying for anyone else.

your enough is too special to taint.
too deep to cut. too magic to defy.
too you to see through.
your enough is boundless.
beyond the beyond.
you are a dream fulfilled.
his dream come true.
you're infinity times enough.
you teach him grace and patience.
he knows love because of your beautiful soul.

the immature magician is l...

unsure of who he is.

the immature magician is lo...

or what he wants.

the immature magician is los...

the good inside him gets overshadowed. he is consumed by a poison that has an antidote but is he man enough to change. to think. to find himself.

the immature magician is lost.

he was taught to be this way.

the mature magician checks his boys when they talk smack.

it is never easy to confront your crew. especially when you have been riding with them for decades. but the mature magician knows the difference between harmful jokes and disrespectful jabs. he checks his boys when they make comments that are demeaning. when they get out of line. when they make comments about you. about your friends. about your relationship. he will shut it down. he is serious about you. your heart.
his crew should know better and more than likely once he says what needs to be said it is no longer an issue. his friends, his people, his family, know he is in it. nothing they say can penetrate what ya'll have. by him taking you serious, they take you serious.

the mature magician is never okay with his boys seeing photos and texts strictly meant for you and he. this is a boundary. the more you keep private the deeper you can go. and he trusts you to do the same. he doesn't share the problems you two may have as gossip but if he confides, he seeks wise council from other men he trusts.

the immature magician is manipulative.

he is highly skilled in the area of deception. slight of hand. slight of heart. slight of mind. the immature magician is manipulative. he maneuvers you. engineers you. steers you. twists you around his finger. works you and is so eloquent he becomes lifeless. emotionless. he doesn't let you into his world because either he questions your motive or has decided long ago to never fall victim to being played. he has decided to always be in control. losing control frightens him. manipulation is not love. it is abusive and harmful. one person is in on the joke while the other is the sacrificial lamb.

the immature magician loves how he was loved. how he was taught to love. how he saw love expressed. when love is always games and tricks and schemes and six degrees seperated from truth he will model what was modeled to him. if manipulation is his foundation, then half-truths contain no truth at all. and you don't deserve to be half-loved.

he was taught to be this way.

commitment
and why he won't fully dedicate himself to you

a man who fails to commit is a man who had little to no man in his life show him what commitment looks like. he knows you are worthy and deserve someone who will be there when the going gets tough but he won't show up. he doesn't know how. not long-term at least. if he can't see himself being with you in the future he will close that door unless he has the mind and heart to try. but by trying he must try with you and only you. if not, he has to be one-hundred percent clear of his intentions and disclose that he plans to talk to you and other people. he can't commit because he never discloses that. especially if he really feels you. digs you. wants you. by declaring that he wants to see you and date other people he stands the chance of losing you. he doesn't want that to happen. so he commits to you but still talks to them. low key. for him, this is the best scenario. but he doesn't clue you in on the fact that he is involved. in the long-run it will not work.

this quasi commitment to you and to himself is his

insurance. a security blanket that enables him to not just have his cake and eat it too, but grants him the ability to water other seeds he has planted.

he won't fully dedicate himself because that would mean letting go of potential relationships he could at some point encounter if the current one doesn't last. and he doesn't want other people courting you so he does just enough to hopefully ensure you're just talking to him while he talks to who knows how many others. this double standard is his playbook. doing to you what he doesn't want done to him.

an honest commitment, one that is deep and full, comes when he wants out of this game. when he chooses to take a step back. to notice how many hearts he has entered. how many hearts he has hurt. how many hearts he has been granted. how many hearts he kept from the ones truly meant for another. how many hearts he wasn't truthful to. how many hearts he broke. how many hearts he could have better appreciated. how many hearts still ache because of him. how many hearts it took for him to come to this realization. once he takes this inventory and comes to grips with the impact of his footprints, he must then choose to not repeat the pattern. he must choose to approach relationship in a more balanced, meausured, and mature way. then and only then will he know and practice commitment.

he was taught to be this way.

the mature magician vanquishes double standards.

what he does you can't do. that's the way it has been but not the way the mature magician lives. how terrible such worlds exist. one where he thinks he reigns supreme and the other he thinks he can rule what you do.

the mature magician exists in-between both. a place where he questions and breaks. not because he wants to be seen as a champion or hero or leader but because unfair treatment of anyone is a fight he deeply feels must be fought. he knows he benefits from double standards and could easily go along. but he uses that language, that insight, that advantage, to probe the world from where he came to show others another side.

you give him the freedom to be. and you also don't let him fall back into that world of human oppression. that world of this and that. that world of he can and you can't. side-by-side you vanquish old models. old ways. old habits. you may not be on a national circuit slaying the system but you inspire others around you to shift.

the immature magician shows you who he's afraid to be.

he plays the part but is in a role. this character is a figment of who you think you need. who you think you need him to be. if you enjoy spending time with family he can do that, too. he will initially go to all the functions. make conversation. show he is caring. willing. consistent. loving. supportive. and your people rave about him. they think he's your match. that you brought a good one home. he passes your test. but once the test has been graded he falls back. into complacency. he can't keep up with the care. because he didn't really care in the first place. he knew what he had to do to get in good graces. if only that attempt wasn't a mask. if it really came from a heart space. if. if. if. if. if. if. if. if. if. he still has you convinced. the immature magician shows you who he's afraid to be.

because he exhausts so much energy being who he isn't, there isn't anything left for you. he becomes irritated quickly. annoyed. demanding. impatient. lazy. stops doing the things you both did together. can't keep up a charade on a house of cards.

the mature magician commits to your soul. when he does that you're the light of his world.

he knows that everything has meaning. when he looks at you he's not thinking of ways to convince you. he is thinking of the moment. thinking how he has waited what may have seemed like forever just to be in your presence so he takes it in. breathes you in. and wants you to feel the moment together. the compliments aren't cliche or in the queue from what he used with others or heard said before. he knows you're an original. you push him to find new words. and by no means is he complaining. you make him better because what he has found in you he has found in him. devotion.

commitment, to the mature magician, is undying. he yields to it. it is part of his purpose compass. like a moth to a flame you are home. a beacon. a reminder. a comfort. a life long life line. the light of his world.

the immature magician tells you *you're what every man wants.*

and then proceeds to use those lines against you. he assumes because other men want you that he is not good enough or that you have options so why would he commit to someone who will eventually find someone better. someone that isn't him. he convinces himself that someone who looks like you, loves like you, feels like you, vibes like you, lives like you, could never fall in love with a man like him.

in his disbelief, fantasy never makes it to reality. and the immature magician dreams more than he lives. he may use these words whenever disagreement comes up or feels under attack or deploys them when he does something wrong and counters with this self-fulfilling prophecy that he can't live up to your expectations anyway. you are what certain people want. what certain people need. but you chose him. it's not on you to convince him. it is on him to understand.

he was taught to be this way.

the mature magician doesn't stray. he stays.

blindsides happen. they come out of nowhere. there is no way to see them coming. no matter how many signs you thought there were. the mature magician is clear with his heart and no matter what, he will verbalize what's going on, where he is, what he wants to do. running away isn't him. isn't within him. if his heart isn't in it you will know. no matter how hard and no matter the hurt he breathes through his emotions.

commitment, for the mature magician, grounds him. it brings him home when it is easiest to stay late where he need not be. it brings him to the voicemail you left on his phone that he saves and checks and checks and checks just to listen. listen. listen. listen. listen. listen.

the home that you have created is always a homecoming. a refuge. a resort. a respite. an intermission. a break from what causes him discomfort. he stays with you because home isn't just a physical place. to him, you are a lifeforce. a mutual strength. an influence. the spirit and energy that fills his soul. you have nothing to prove to him because together you fit. you fit. you fit.
you fit. he stays. doesn't stray.

the immature magician's promises are empty. incomplete. strategies for you to hold on to him.

a mack is someone who is slick. smooth. a seam you can't see. he is romanticized. glorified. looked up to. not for honorable reasons. for collecting bodies. for being deemed unreachable. always getting away. never held accountable. never in trouble. the rule. not the exception. master of deception.

he is cool. a role model. a jester disguised. hollow. lonely. his promises are empty. he doesn't know how to fulfill them. the immature magician has a way with velvet red carpet words. this doesn't mean you are gullible. it means your heart is open. you have no reason to assume ill intent. his strategy is to do as little work as possible. to give as little love as he can. just enough to not be suspected. with every broken promise he apologizes. says he will change. he won't.

LOVER

thelover
archetype

he must learn to love
how he learned to walk
let him fall and get back up
love is a language misunderstood
at his core he believes it makes him soft
too stubborn to let go
too armoured to know
and when he opens up
the light will come in
the love will begin to heal
his fractured soul
please understand
how he responds
is out of deep wound
but it's not an excuse
he can *he must* do better & become his best version
the lover in him works on his walls to come down
the lover in him gives himself permission to feel
the lover in him shows his big heart
the lover in him honors the lover in you

he was taught to be this way.

emotionallystagnant
and why he fears digging to the root of his hurt

acknowledgment makes situations real. attention. thought. voice. all require honesty. truth that can't be hidden behind. he has to be in a place to face why he is hurt. men who haven't done soul work have a hard time pinpointing the source. the root. the first time he gave of himself completely and heartache struck. instead. his behavior reflects the unnamed pain. does things that keep you from getting too close to feel his sunlight.

running away in place, keeping his past behind him, creates more distance between him and his heart. his core connection to the lover within him.

honoring that broken part of him takes the right amount of compassion. the right amount of love. not just on your behalf if you're the one with the desire to unlock this trauma. but on his behalf. he must love himself enough to dig and uncover the walls. he must empathize deep enough to avoid judging himself and trust the process as it develops.

heartache is painful. especially for those who have trouble letting people in. but for him, there was a time it was easier. he was tender and believed in the beauty of love and relationships.

once. more than once. he gave undivided adoration to one and only one person. he informed the others that he appreciated the moments they had together but has since moved on and seeing someone. exclusively. this was a new approach for him. informing. being transparent. he could have told them things that they could hold onto. but he cut it off. respectfully. he did the right thing.

he took a risk once. more than once.

he let you in on his past. his secrets. his hurt. his work. his never-told-anyone-else-before ghosts that crept into other situations. and then, it didn't work out. for whatever reason. but this time, it wasn't his fault. he cared. more. he tried. hard. fell. in love. the kind of love that moved him like nothing before.

but remembering that part of his life means he must again admit and experience a deep loss. relive heartache. and to dig that deep, admitting he's still wounded, is scary. it can trigger emotions that get him stuck. he's stagnant but there's hope.

he was taught to be this way.

the mature lover is a gentle man.

kind. tender. sympathetic. considerate. understanding. compassionate. these are some of the words linked with the term gentle. the mature lover's attitude and actions are aligned and calibrate in a way that can be felt. his energy is calm. his language is soft and strong.

he is soft. soft. soft.

soft is way of connecting to the feminine. his own femininity does not undermine his masculinity. he is man enough. mature enough. to know that he is soft and strong. man and woman. both and. when he sits and acknowledges his emotions he engages his water. his woman. his power. his source. his ability to do this allows him to see you. to breathe with you. to get back to equilibrium.

this connection. this vibe. this way of life. isn't passive. isn't less manly. isn't gendered. isn't pitted up against a societal norm. gentle is one of his guiding stars. a north star. a marker. to return to his grounding. to return to a kind of love where gravity doesn't exist. the gentle man is a gentle lover. a gentle soul.

the immature lover is a rebounder.

he feeds off of being needed. indulges and jumps at the opportunity when wounded hearts come his way. a sad past and a sad story offer a way in to show that his shoulder is yours to cry on. the immature lover plagues on sorrow. it gives him advantage. a false sense of pedastol he has gifted himself. he sees you as a match. not his match. but as game. to overcome. to accomplish. to lure you into thinking he has the answer. has the means to make you feel better. has the needle to sew the tears. has the hands that wipe your tears. this isn't empathy. he's there for the rebound not the rim. not the court. not the arena.

when he catches you at your lowest he will handle you with care. he knows how. but he won't feel with you. he won't deeply invest. he plays with others. one too many. he is splitting his energy between you and his squad. players on his team that you don't know about. when it gets real the immature lover subs you out. then if he needs you, he will sub you back in.

he sees you filling a role. you are a role player. and your job (to him) is to not catch on to the game.

he was taught to be this way.

the mature lover digs deep into his heart & figures out how he is feeling. all the time.

"why doesn't he share with me how he feels? do i not prompt enough? do i not show him how i feel well enough to show him i care?"

the mature lover is quick to detect slight changes in his mood and has enough awareness about himself that he can avoid (or prepare for) things that trigger him. digging deep is uncomfortable but he takes the time to turn that discomfort as fuel that tells him he's feeling some kind of way. it may take him some time to name the source or figure out why, but he gets there. and sometimes he won't share how he feels because he doesn't feel safe psychologically. this means that there may be some fear of negative consequences by speaking his truth. he'd rather have what he shares be cared for and not sharpened to be used to stab him in his back. if he knows you feel adversely, he's protecting himself first and will tell you he's doing so.

the immature lover is disconnected from his heart. he's not just hiding, he's isolating.

"why do men choose to hide their feelings or act like things aren't bothering them when they are?"

his feelings are his currency. the more he gives out the less he has left. and the more he divulges the more ammunition you have against him. at least this is how he sees it. opening up ain't easy. if it was, every man would do it and this world would look and feel very different. the immature lover will play it off like all things are cool because he's not going to make a big deal out of something that will eventually make him talk. make him sit with the fire in his belly. so instead he puts his feelings in a box. he's gotten so good at isolating himself from himself, that he has become desensitized. the more he avoids the less equipped he becomes at pinpointing what will eventually set him off. he assumes how he feels will go away. but it is bottling up. he is disconnected from his heart.

the mature lover listens to his heart.

he is trained to solve problems using love and logic.
using logic only half serves him. this makes him
incomplete. but love and logic permit him to access
better fullness. a complete kind of breath that guides
him to better understanding. better grounding. clarity
visits the mature lover more often when he listens to
his heart. when he opens himself to the vast ocean
of emotions that visit him. so you, beloved, need not
worry if you're too much for him. it is enough.
your love isn't too intimidating for him.
your love isn't too strong for him.
your love for him lets him know you are real.
that your love is undivided. that your love
tells it like it is. that your love, like his love,
has an unforseen depth that both of you
courageously dive down into.
him not leading.
you not following.
taking turns
vibing
reclaiming
what making love
really means.

the immature lover memorizes his lines. using the same words over and over and over and over again.

i don't want to talk, not in the mood right now, nothing is wrong, leave me alone, i just want to play my game, i told you i'm good, you always want to have a conversation, the game is on, i don't want to fight, i have nothing to say, we're good, i hear you, what do you want me to say?...

subconscious. unthoughtful. quick responses to get out of having dialogue. you might just want to simply connect and spend time but when he just wants some alone time the immature lover doesn't know how to communicate effectively so it comes off brash and rigid. "can we talk" or "i want to talk to you about something" registers in his head as "what did i do now" and "here we go again" and "i'm tired of talking about my past" — clearly he isn't listening.

he was taught to be this way.

the mature lover lets you in and protects your heart.

his love for you started the moment he first heard the sound of your words. your language and how your energy emphasized what was most important set you apart. you cut through the noise. because this time he didn't center himself as hero. this time he centered himself as learner. a wanderer seeking a guide. not a teacher to teach him or mold him or set him on the right path. but a human willing to accept the sins of a man looking to come clean — the mature lover seeks a new way. the way of the lover. the way of love. the way to love. to allow the flow of love to cover him. to fill him. to invite him. to encourage him. to root him. the way of the lover is the protection of other lovers and their most prized possession — their heart.

a lovers mantra:

when she lets you in protect her heart.

when he lets you in protect his heart.

the immature lover believes violence is love.

violence in any form is never okay. used as a distressed means to maintain power and control, the immature lover will say things like *i'm doing this because i love you.* or gift you something asking for pardon and forgiveness in hopes to undo the damage he has done. masking behavior in this way is despicable and abusive.

physical violence is not love.
sexual violence is not love.
emotional violence is not love.
psychological violence is not love.
spiritual violence is not love.
cultural violence is not love.
verbal violence is not love.
financial violence is not love.
neglectful violence is not love.

violence is not love. withholding and/or manipulating someone against their will is downright evil.

communication

& opening up is the most masculine thing he can do

vulnerability is giving your all.
it says
this is uncomfortable but i'm trusting you with what
i'm carrying within.
it means
i'm not perfect. i'm a bit of a mess.
and i need you to listen without judgement.
it feels
scary. ***real love means being committed to doing
what is hard in order to grow.***

men can be vulnerable.
men can be vulnerable.
men can be vulnerable.
men can be vulnerable.
men can be vulnerable.
men can be vulnerable.
men can be vulnerable.

if he practices vulnerability he will see how light it
makes him feel. it is terrifying but it shouldn't be.

*"the guys i know are always the worst at communication and
a lot of fights and drama happens because of their inability to
express emotions or be honest. they know in today's society that
it is fine but they still struggle with it..."*

men communicate. they just do it in ways that can be confusing and evasive. whether his style is passive, aggressive, or passive-agressive often times he isn't as clear as you'd want him to be. asserting and expressing his own desires, thoughts and feelings is the ideal and most effective form of communication but it relies on knowing what he wants and why he responds the way that he does. there is a reason he doesn't open up and tell his truth. go deeper.

sentence starters to help him open up (4 quarter communication in sequence*)

"this is what happened/this is what's going on..." (the story)
"i think..." (thoughts about what happened/what's going on)
"i feel..." (feelings about what happened/what's going on)
"what i want..." (expectations/desires moving forward)

in practice it might look like this:

*"**this is what happened**: yesterday you were on my page and
asked me why i was following certain accounts on instagram.
i think you shouldn't worry about who i follow because i don't
care who you are following. **i feel** like you don't trust me and that
makes me angry and sad. **i want** to be in a trusting relationship.*

**before moving on to the next quarter (what happened/thoughts/feelings/wants) give as much
information until you are complete e.g. "i think" could have several sentences. say them all before going into "i feel". after one person goes (without being interrupted) the other can respond.*

he was taught to be this way.

the mature lover accepts how what he does impacts you.

he hears you. every word that leaves your mouth. and every gesture your body makes when words aren't able to tell him what's bothering you. he knows when he causes you frustration. take the instagram example from the last page. his response may have come right after you asked why he follows certain pages or some time may have gone by. but it doesn't stop there.

although what he tells you is honest (he has every right to feel the way that he feels) that doesn't mean he is shut off from the impact the situation has on you. so when you respond by saying:

"i notice that you follow accounts with women who are barely wearing any clothes. every picture they post they are basically naked. i think you like looking at other women. i think you don't care how that makes me feel. i feel like i'm not enough for you and that makes me feel insecure. i want you to be more considerate and be aware of how that comes off."

listening to that, being open to that feedback, hits home for the mature lover. he adjusts accordingly.

the immature lover can't be vulnerable.

because he doesn't know what it means.

vul·ner·a·ble, *adj*. **1**. capable of or susceptible to being physically, spiritually, emotionally wounded or hurt. **2**. open to criticism. **3**. willing to admit fault and blame. **4**. speaking truth / being truthful. **5**. freedom to feel. **6**. comfort to share and spill the soul. **7**. caring about things deeply. **8**. ability to be courageously honest with self and others. **9**. unguarded openness.

distancing himself from vulnerability disconnects him from a universe of possibilities. to freely express what is on his mind and how he truly feels is foreign. being vulnerable when he doesn't know how can show a dent in his ability so he has mastered his way to get around things by just saying *this is who i am*. what he is really saying: *accept the things that i am doing*.

the immature lover's instagram response would be:

"..."

"i mean if you feel that way why are you even with me? i'd hope you'd be secure enough with yourself to not worry about this stuff."

// doesn't even care.

the mature lover doesn't bottle up. he practices **being vulnerable** which makes him an even better man.

vulnerability doesn't always call for being an open book ready and willing to express how you feel to others. it is an awareness and greater understanding of simply observing how the body responds to certain questions, situations, emotions, and naming the level of comfort. the mature lover knows not to bottle up and contain his inside world because it instructs his outside world behaviors and interactions.

he is unguarded and recognizes the strength it takes to lean into his vulnerable power. being more emotionally literate makes him a better man, a better husband, a better father, a better friend, a better whole person.

the immature lover shrinks.

it's not that
he can't
it's that
he won't
look
at
himself
see
for himself
why
why
why
why
why
he
shrinks
when
the
v
word
touches
his
spine.

he was taught to be this way.

gratitude
as a practice, a guide, a breath

gratitude goes beyond a fleeting feeling. it is on-going. when men tap into intentional reflection of what they have, who they have, where they've been, and how they feel, they initiate a process of change. being grateful does not rely on someone telling you what to do. the state of being grateful is a conscious choice to step beyond yourself and bring awareness to the very things that are ignored and overlooked.

gratitude is a purposeful thank you.
it is a necessary practice that takes time.
takes energy. takes courage. to step into
vulnerability and find reasons why you
should be grateful. especially when
telling someone what they did for you or
writing down emotions or just thinking
and meditating can cause discomfort.

men must actively decide to be consistent with their gratitude practice. to mature. to flourish. to advance deep into feeling. to become the feeling. to not

vanish like a quick word of thanks but to actually
sit with that appreciation. appreciation isn't always
easy. like when you're in an argument and distance
is preferable. when you're fuming and want nothing
to do with them. or you're in a moment of anxiety
and can't seem to control your attitude or are frantic
walking back and forth not knowing what to do
and a loved one tells you to take a breath to help
calm you down. or someone you've been with for a
while breaks up with you and you wholeheartedly
believed they were the one and you ache all over.

there are lessons in all of those scenarios.

do this for five minutes.
find a quiet place. inside or out in nature.
sit comfortably on a chair, or on the ground.
close your eyes or keep them open.
be still. pay attention to your breath.
inhale as long as you want. exhale.
repeat as many times as you need.
think about what you are grateful for.
say it to yourself silently or out loud.

do this once a day.
get out your journal. in the morning or at night.
close your eyes. take a breath. reflect. write.
write down three things you are grateful for.
bullet points or in complete sentences.

the mature lover
is grateful for you.

all the things you do. the little things. the big things.
the things in-between. he is grateful. and he shows it.

gratitude
for the mature lover
are love notes
scribbled phrases
private prayers
drives alone
walks to contemplate
anything
that gives him space
to acknowledge
how far he has come
how far he has to go
and to give homage
through sincere
appreciation
for you   *he is grateful*
for you   *for you because*
for you   *he gets to begin*
for you   *anew each day*
for you.   *next to you.*

the immature lover doesn't understand why he should be grateful for you but will make sure you show gratitude towards him.

the worst kinds of people know what it takes to make someone feel bad for not being overjoyed or express jubilation when they give them something. if the response doesn't exceed the expecation of excitement, amazement, humility or graciousness then he might feel disrespected as if you were being ungrateful. as if you didn't appreciate him. being with him. he may even throw it in your face that he could be with someone who is more grateful as ploy that puts the relationship at risk. he doesn't understand how gratitude works. if he did he'd appreciate you more.

he was taught to be this way.

sex
the measuring stick for manhood

sex is a game of thrones. the goal to achieve at the end of a date. conversation among immature men quickly measures the success of your time together with questions like *did she give it up, did you get any, how long do you think she will make you wait.* these talks get pointier and competitive if indeed he didn't "get any" as someone will often always say something about if they were out with her they would have been hit it and smashed. jokes about how he failed and probably didn't try hard enough will further drown any emphasis on getting to know the person but focus in on conquering her person.

those who see sex as tournament fail to recognize how serious a contract it is. engaging in it requires a sincere understanding that joining in this way will forever bind us. that we are exchanging parts of us in such intimacy that must be entered into with care.
the moment temporary
the energy imprints established
the soul tie everlasting.

yet he is taught that this union that intertwines people is no big deal. that sex is what makes you cool. makes you a man. that sex is what a woman wants. that her body is all the attention he looks for.

sex is the way in which men were raised to express love. sex is the way in which men were taught to communicate how they feel. sex is the way in which men share a sense of belonging. sex is the way in which men define relationships.

sex is sacred. it brings new life. not to take lightly and play with. girls are taught that sex matters, that it is this beautiful thing to be patient and wait. but for boys it is something to take. to get good at. to master. an unfortunate measuring stick for manhood. too much concern is placed on his penis size causing pressure to perform, please and last.

sex and sexuality encompasses physical, emotional, spiritual, social, mental, energetic, and psychological dimensions. being more aware of this awakens and deepens all relations with self and others. it isn't just about getting off and releasing which oversimplifies sexual process and activity. to spend time in and out of sex, extends the conversation about true intimacy and connection. understanding that having sex isn't always physical is a liberatory act and is a beautiful labor of love.

he was taught to be this way.

the mature lover knows how to connect without having sex.

"can couples create a deep non-sexual connection?"

there is something there that is felt. beyond the skin. underneath bloodstream speechless words. a humming that sits in your belly. comfortable. uncomfortable. telling you there is something there. between you. but you can't call it. you can't name it. and the mature lover has mastered not needing to label it as anything but chemistry. magic. energy. that flows between you. this emotional wavelength outweighs any desire to ruin it with physical handprints. this tie is a long sigh and a deep breath. he doesn't confuse it with trying to seduce or prey. he decodes it by asking if you are feeling it too. a sensation that draws you into the water together. to explore. to probe. to wonder. but not decide. to sit. and get closer. he doesn't need sex to be the answer. emotional love is a revolution. a healing act. to go against the current. can couples create a deep non-sexual connection? yes. but it must be communicated in advance or the two of you will never be satisfied. he listens with his whole being not what's between his legs.

the immature lover has a high sex count.

"why can men partake in whatever and however many sexual endeavors they please, and get high-fived for it? a woman who does the same gets shamed."

this is the double standard. him to play and be rewarded and she to be shamed and discarded. the gameboard of sex has always been male dominated.

for him. it's just about sex. no emotional connection. he doesn't know how it is impacting his psyche or his soul or how he will wound future relationships. for that will be the hardest thing to unlearn. to see sex as the totality of expression beyond touching. for what it may mean to turn her on won't always mean bedroom or to showcase what he is working with. but to open his heart and share what is on his mind. to make love with words and loving touch versus a quickie.

too often the urge is to lean into that feeling thinking it calls for physical behavior when in fact it should be dealt with on the emotional level. the immature lover misunderstands because he only speaks one language. and a high sex count proves that he is the man.

the mature lover is confident in his skin and sexuality. saying *i love you* is normal.

sexuality is not talked about enough. more than likely if ever discussed it is on a spectrum that places straight on one end and gay on the other. but the mature lover knows that sexuality is in fact based on many levels and layers that remind him that anything on the binary is a false dichotomy meant only to divide. he knows there is no need to assume that showing affinity and love to another man need not mean anything sexual. that it is needed and normal to tell another man that you love them. and mean it. with no need to laugh or joke or diminish it in any way. that part of being his brother's keeper is in fact obligatory to affirm him and honor him and support him. and to hug and to dap and to say i love you and to talk deeply with one another and to to check-in and to show up and to cry with and to laugh with and to lean on one another is the strongest kind of love that makes him a man. it's healthy and natural to give and receive mans love without stigmatizing it and marginalizing its impact and significance.

the immature lover cringes at anything that has anything to do with sexuality.

everything that is questionable and breaches into sensitivity, emotions, care and love towards men is always blunted with the modifier: *no homo* or *pause*. as a means to distance himself to being seen as coming onto or encroaching upon it coming off as gay. this is the problem with the immature lover. anything that is not manly or anything that broaches feminine energy probably makes him cringe. this is because he has always been told and has always been taught and has always been reminded that there are certain things that men must certainly not do in order to stay in the man box. to stay in the green. this hardens him. this controls him. and if and when he happens upon or spends time with men who may like men makes him very uncomfortable. he assumes that they are into him. will try to hit on him. he pushes them further away into the terrible stereotype without really considering this to be untrue. and rather than being comfortable in his own sexuality he threatens the safety of other men.

OPEN
LETTERS

he was taught to be this way.

dear son
an open letter to your heart

when you are older i hope you will stumble across these pages. and fall into these words. this manual. not as truth or as the only or as a past time. but to be critical and introspective and as a guide for us. who knows, perhaps most of this will be outdated and you will share new insights. new reasons. new versions. and will re-write this. respond to this.

one thing, to be clear, i hope you remember this. raising you i have always been conscious about the language i use. what i say. how i say it. my behavior. what i do. why i do it. and when you cry and fall and express i always always always ask:

are you okay? it's okay if you're not okay.

literally. every time. and most times you will say:

yes.

and sometimes you will say *no*. and that you want

my help. and you extend your hand and in your two-year-old voice say, "hep peez" as you sit on the ground waiting for me to assist. those are the beautiful moments, just like that, that i want you to hold on to. to ask for help when you need it. to try first to help yourself. to struggle a bit. first. but when you feel stuck and have no way through to reach and check-in with community. with a friend. a teacher. a mentor. me. your mom. about other ways to help unstick you. i never want you to think you have to do things on your own. to keep things inside. i don't want you to hold fear anywhere near you. i want you to be free to explore all of your humanity and to thrive in all of your identities.

son. come to me. always. forever. for whatever. with uncertainty. with anxiety. with sadness. with anger. with delight. with harmony. with tears. with you. with whatever you are holding. i may never have an answer. but i'll have a shoulder. the time. the heart. the mirror. to see you. to support you. to listen. to listen. to listen. to listen. and to give what you may not know you need. to hold you. to hug you. to kiss you. to laugh with you. to fuss at. to silence with. to beer with. to golden state warriors with. to be with. i'm your guy. always. forever. for whatever. i'm already so proud of the happy human you are. the kind and loving and funny and gentle soul you give the world. thank you son. i love you.

dear man

an open letter to your heart

allowing yourself to be uncomfortable is where growth happens. and there have been times (i hope) in this volume where you closed it. where you shook your head. where you sighed. where you leaned in. and kept going instead of stopping. this is your work. your burden. your task. to crack wide open. to get expansive. to get expressive. to get vulnerable. at whatever level you need to start at. and to keep going. to probe and probe and probe and probe and probe. there is too much at stake. what you need to hear is that you gotta do better. and this could be that step. that choice. that move. to move. to check yourself. perfection is not anywhere in sight. that isn't real or the purpose or the intention. you are good. you hear me? you are incredible. but understand this: you can and need to be better. to model. to undo. unmask. unearth. unlearn. everything. every little nuance. to lay it all out in front of yourself and wonder why wonder who wonder where wonder how wonder what every lesson has ever crossed your path and test it. examine it. press it. and if it is useful keep it. if it isn't drop it. and get others to drop it too. this isn't quick or fast or a check in the box. it is a sojourn back to where you've been running from and unknowingly not even knowing you were running away from this. this is not the gospel. this is the gap. the hole. for you to face. to take a look and forge your truth. this is not blame or guilt or shame or embarrasment or belittle or disrespect. this is a gift. a tiny footnote. to inhale. and i hope you would trust me enough to know that i care about you enough and love you enough to hold your feet to this fire. to contain your wounds and to catch your fall. to clasp and crash and deny and cry and push and pull and fumble and fumble and fumble and fumble. with you. can't do this alone. you hear me? it isn't possible. deep down you know this but you have been taught to hold yourself down and accept no help as long as you can. to pretend and to front and to resist feeling. this is your call. to read this again. to take sharpie and post-its and notepad and pencil and partner to unravel and re-work this. to scribe your own volume. to rip this to shreds and to combine your experience and perspective and reason and soul to tell your story. to display your side. your struggles. now is the time to fill in this gap. to prepare the harvest within. i am taking you to task. dear brother. to charge and promise yourself and the men in your circle to talk and respond truthfully about what you were taught.

he was taught to be this way.

dear man. i see you. i see you. i see you. i see you. i see you. i see you. i see you. i see you. i see you. i see you. i see you. i see you. i see you. i see you.

i honor that part of you that believes and knows that you are inherently good. well-intentioned. kind. sincere. loving. helpful. direct. honest. trust-worthy. law-abiding. balanced. the list can go on. i see you. and i also see parts of you that limits you. that bothers you. that scares you. that hardens you. that hurts you. and i want more from you. more for you. to acknowledge when and if you are too heavy on the toxic/unhelpful/immature side of things. to bear witness to the feedback a loved one gives. to take it in. to breathe it in. to breathe it in. to breathe it in. and to know that you are human and are capable to adjust and to plunge. but don't wait. alright? don't hold this off. you have this in your hands so clearly this is a start or a continuation of your journey to over expose where you have been. why you are. how you are. when you are. what you are. who you are. you can grow outwardly but what about inward growth? inner healing. inner being. what can you commit to doing right now right now right now right now not later. this isn't a "man take lead" kind of plead. this is a "man go deep" to the deep end kind of invitation. you got everything you need. to equilibrium. to simply ask why and give yourself permission to take the time to find the source. to not stop there but to keep going. to say *yeah i was taught to be this way but i'm learning to do and be and think and feel something differently*. in solidarity. in love. in peace. cool runnings man.

he was taught to be this way.

dear woman
an open letter to your heart

it is not on your shoulders to make men better.
it is not on your shoulders to make men better.
it is not on your shoulders to make men better.
it is not on your shoulders to make men better.
it is not on your shoulders to make men better.
it is not on your shoulders to make men better.
it is not on your shoulders to make men better.
it is not on your shoulders to make men better.
it is not on your shoulders to make men better.
it is not on your shoulders to make men better.
it is not on your shoulders to make men better.
it is not on your shoulders to make men better.
it is not on your shoulders to make men better.
it is not on your shoulders to make men better.
it is not on your shoulders to make men better.
it is not on your shoulders to make men better.
it is not on your shoulders to make men better.
it is not on your shoulders to make men better.
it is not on your shoulders to make men better.
it is not on your shoulders to make men better.
it is not on your shoulders to make men better.
it is not on your shoulders to make men better.
it is not on your shoulders to make men better.

you are a reason we must right our wrongs. and you can help but you can not lead a man to do anything he hasn't set in his heart to overcome. this is fact. you can help him see and help him peel and help him analyze but there will be no change in him or change around him until he chooses the shift. the path. the new way. this doesn't take you off the hook or even place you on a hook. for you have been helping man do his work while doing yours for one second too long. one relationship too many. one wound too many. one expectation too many. this may sound hollow but i am truly sorry. on behalf of myself. i can't and will not speak for other men. there is harm in that. but there is genuine in this: *i am sorry* for the conscious and unconsious things i have ever done that was at your expense. was at your tears. was at your heartache. was at my childish. i didn't know. but i knew. and this may not get to any root or recovery or absolution but i need you to know that this man (and many others) sees you. appreciates you. loves you. loves you. loves you. loves you. and yet we fail you time and again. for our own stuff we haven't prioritized to therapy. to stop. to care deep enough to be brave to truly partner to relationship to align with. on the small and big things you tell us we need to reflect on. dear woman. this whole piece is more than a project. it is a process. commandment to go beyond try and practice the do. to let go of the rock and study why we (i) (us) held

he was taught to be this way.

and hold onto what we've been holding so long. dear woman. you aren't the lid. you aren't the lid. you aren't the lid. it is not on your shoulders to make men better. you deserve more than the pain that has been bundled with half-love no-love semi-love false-love immature-love. you deserve so much more. you deserve everything you bar you expect you give in return in what you sacrifice. and as you yourself go through hardship and happiness and all that is between i hope men in your life help lift you as you climb as you soar as you become who you set to be who you are meant to be. for men to help create bridges and side with you to combat barriers. dear woman. thank you.

grandmother. mother. sister. neice. friend. wife. auntie. half sister. great grand mother. step mother. daughter. super woman. mother earth. queen mother. cousin. mother-in-law. daughter-in-law. sister-in-law. all of you (like us) are breathing this air. among this fog. and have an important role in pushing back. in dismantling. unlearning. educating. raising. holding space for what boyhood and manhood looks like. it is in what you say how you say it why you say it that is key in the development of everyone. how can you disrupt the system? how can you examine your teachings and commit to those you knowingly and unknowingly come across feel an embrace of you seeing them without saying anything. is it part of your responsibility. your task. to observe and to step in and to recalibrate and to push and to push and to push more and more and more and breathe and breathe and breathe with us. for us. through us. by us. for you.

if you do only one thing i hope it is this. you still with me? i want you to keep faith. to keep hope. to expect that we get our shit together. for us, as men, to lead ourselves back to the beautiful waters you wombed us and bathed us and tided us in. this is (again) on us to come back to center and let go let go let go let go of the problematic and restore. dear woman. i said a lot of things and this note might be too long and too wordy and too out there and for that i leave you with one last line: this man sees you. loves you. hears you.

dear wife
an open letter to your heart

you often ask why i do the things that i do. i never have the answer as i am still in search for the deeper reasons why. this is an attempt to expose you more insight. not to release me from conversation but to provide greater context as i continue to learn and grow. as i continue to stumble and flashlight and stutter and plant and repeat. out of everything i have written in these pages these words exclusively have been the hardest. for how can a writer such as myself conduct an arrangement of letters and offer up sense to the one who is foundational. this is horrid attempt. but by now i hope you have seen the budding of a man striving to be somewhat better each day. and i relapse. we all do. and i admit i am not easy but you make loving you easy. your clarity and earnest desire to communicate is bedrock. and tho i try to avoid the hotseat you lovingly and patiently give me the space and time and gently (or roughly) nudge me to do the hard stuff. to talk when i want to hold in. to talk when i want to avoid. to deep when i want to shallow. to courage when i want to numb. dear wife. you are everything. every thing. every blessing. every lesson. every gift. you've had to endure and resist and break through and restrain and remind and trench and birth and grind and hurt and bloom and wall and and and. and through it all you love. you love. you love. you love. still. so unbreakable you are. no matter what. i'm just thankful. grateful. appreciative. of you. for you. with you. by you. i am because of you. you're the best teacher best healer best holder best gardener best wanderer best mother best creator. the greatest whatever and wherever there is. you (dearest wife) deserve to be woman of the year. woman of the universe. woman of the soul. these words are yours. and as we both navigate and figure and bruise and bump and master, it is my plea that this be a working document. to anchor us. to course us. and to tighten us. for i see all the work you've been doing getting to know yourself. why-ing yourself. re-discovering yourself. as a mom. as a wife. as a friend. as a daughter. as a sister. as a creative. as a designer. as a human. and it is inspiring. and terrifying. to be in space with someone already in the fire. dear wife. you complete me when i am whole. you complete me when i am half. you complete me when i feel like i am or have nothing left to give. i am because of you. i do not say this enough. i love you hbbc.

dear self
an open letter to your heart

by no means is this a pat on the back. but it is important for you to recognize your effort your heart your courage your work. on this. too often you overlook and downplay and dismiss the magnitude of what you gift and offer and give. you poured. and prodded. and persisted. to get this done. this was never to be self-serving but it became self-help. for this to work you had to be raw and real and if no one reads this that is okay because now you have a handbook that didn't exist when you needed it. and there were many moments (many many) you stopped writing this because it got to be too hard. too emotional. too unnerving. to sometimes see yourself in the text in the questions in the why in the toxic. for your feet to be held in the fire. i honor you. i'm proud of you. for you are still learning and unlearning. still wondering still processing. you aren't all-knowing and do not claim to be. but what i know to be true is that you've opened up something that has been locked for way too long. use this collection. lean on this. re-write this. love.

dear all
an open letter to your heart

it takes a village. all of us. everyone. to do this work. to be in community. to learn. to heal. this is real life. our life. for now. for those that come after. it is on our backs and our hands and our hearts and our minds and our souls to collectively toil and re-soil. re-plant. re-administer. re-apply. key ingredients that allows space for everyone to be. to lead happy meaningful purposeful fulfilled lives. of course there will be obstacles and conflict and drama and problems but at what cost. does someone always have to be the target. how can we guide the youth to their fullest potential if they have to distance themselves from parts of their core. this is for our boys. in particular. not because they matter most. but because i cannot write any other book that isn't my lived experience. that is for someone else. to invite me. to invite us. so this joint is for our fathers. uncles. brothers. nephews. cousins. step dads. sons. husbands. great and grand fathers. the in-laws. lovers. magicians. warriors. kings. this isn't the ending. simply the beginning.

he was taught to be this way.

HWTTBTW.
II

BY ADRIAN MICHAEL
NOW AVAILABLE

Made in the USA
Columbia, SC
06 January 2020